CW00347283

best friends

Sandra Deeble

with photography by Dan Duchars

best friends

RYLAND
PETERS
& SMALL
LONDON NEW YORK

For my life coach, Sarah Ridgard

Designer Catherine Griffin
Editor Miriam Hyslop
Location Research Claire Hector
Picture Research Emily Westlake
Production Deborah Wehner
Art Director Gabriella Le Grazie
Publishing Director Alison Starling

First published in the
United Kingdom in 2003
by Ryland Peters & Small
Kirkman House
12–14 Whitfield Street
London W1T 2RP
www.rylandpeters.com

10 9 8 7 6 5 4 3 2 1

ISBN 1 84172 391 6

A CIP record for this book is available
from the British Library.
Printed and bound in China

contents

life support

Where would we be without our female friends?

When everything seems to be going wrong – your relationship is falling apart at the seams; you've put in an offer on a house but now you're wondering whether there's any point; and now, all of a sudden, your job is looking decidedly dodgy, who do you turn to? Your friends. They'd do anything for you, and you for them. They've seen you in any number of difficult situations over the years. You know that just picking up the phone and talking to one of them will make you feel better. As Marlene Dietrich once said: 'It's the friends that you can call at 4am that matter.' How true! Just knowing that they're there and that you can count on them makes a difference.

You can even anticipate what they might say to cheer you up; you start to feel a bit better before you have even spoken to them! So who exactly do you call at 4am? Well, that might depend on what the problem is. Flippancy aside, we all have different friends for different occasions. There's Relationships Friend. Career Adviser Friend. Stand-Up Comedienne Friend. No Nonsense Friend. And of course, some friends have the knack of being able to multi-task. When you're at a total loss, your close friends understand you even when you're finding it difficult to express how you're feeling. A good friend with whom you share an almost sisterly closeness gives you strength, confidence and hope. What would we do without our friends?

communication

experts

The joy of communicating

Female friends need little encouragement when it comes to fulfilling their need to communicate something the very moment it happens. You need advice but your friend is on the phone? Call her mobile. It's switched off? Send her an email. You're in a meeting but you desperately want to know if your best friend has gone into labour. Ask her partner to send you a text message. As for being on a blind date: when he goes to the bar, the temptation to give your friend an update – in real time – is simply irresistible. Just make sure that you don't get caught!

More seriously, if a close friend ups sticks to go and live overseas, you're devastated, but email will prove to be a great healer. New technology is perfect when you want instant gratification. Yet there are countless times when sending a card really hits the spot. Many of us have filled treasure chests – or shoe boxes – over the years with cherished notes from friends sent at both the most hellish and joyous times in our lives. Looking back at them is like reading our  own diary. 'Was I really feeling like that?' Our friends provide another perspective on our memories. One of the great pleasures of female friendship is being confident that you can contact them at any time, you don't need a reason.

girls' night in

All the girls together

'Why don't you come round? We'll order a pizza and get out *Bridget Jones's Diary* on video.' Or failing that why not eat comfort food — sticky toffee pudding and real vanilla ice cream — while settling in to repeats of *Sex and the City*, *Friends*, or *ER*? Our unalloyed delight at the prospect of spending a night in with the girls must stem from our memories of pyjama

parties, midnight feasts in boarding schools — even if we only read about them — or just being allowed to sleep over at our best friend's house. So often, we have the best fun with our friends without leaving home. Staying in is, after all, the new going out.

Yet it has always been this way. Kitchen tables are where the really good chats take place. You can be busy cooking while your friend regales you with her latest tale of passion as you both drink for England. When we're with our female friends we have a unique ability to jump from the most trivial

Happiness seems made to be shared.

Jean Racine

conversations to the deepest analysis. It's a very well practised skill! And just when you thought you'd temporarily lost your bestest friend as she disappears into a bubble-gum cloud of post-honeymoon bliss, her husband goes off to do something sporty, or indulge in another male bonding activity. All of a sudden, there she is, organizing a weekend with the girls. The hens reunite – and it's as if nothing has changed!

When it's all girls together, the complete openness, the let-it-all hang-out-ness and propensity for belly laughing is a complete tonic. Whether you're stressed because you work too hard, you're exhausted from looking after your children or you feel you're becoming too addicted to Do-It-Yourself, a night in with the girls can take years off you. It's official: it's good for your health! 'Laughter glues us together,' is how one woman describes her circle of friends. They've known each other for 16 years and they now refer to themselves as the Ya-Yas — inspired by reading Rebecca Wells's book *Divine Secrets of the Ya-Ya Sisterhood*. 'Oh my god, that's us!' one of them said. Marriage and children have not come in the way of these Ya-Yas. There are five of them and they see each other every couple of weeks. They even go on holiday together, and now that one of them has gone to live in France,

> *When friends meet,*
> *hearts warm.*

Proverb

her home has become the Ya-Yas' new holiday destination. 'We've helped each other through loads of stuff,' she says, 'boyfriends, houses, jobs. We've never fallen out. It's really healthy. We take it in turns to host our get-togethers. We eat, drink and catch up on what everyone's been doing. We always laugh from the minute we're together. We know we're really lucky. It's fantastic. The Ya-Yas give another dimension to my life. They're like a different kind of family to me.'

girls' night out

'Do you want to get ready here?'

This is a question we start asking our female friends early on in our lives. Going out after school, you might go to a friend's house first. Later, the 'getting ready to hit the town' ritual can become increasingly time-consuming. It's no longer a question of changing out of your school uniform into something more flattering. We're talking about serious pampering and transformation! It can take even longer than the preparation for a hot date. All of a sudden, you've got more clothes to try on, and replacing the mirror is a panel of people you can ask: 'Does my bum look big in this?' And you really trust your friends to be brutally honest — don't you? However you go about it, getting ready together can set you up for a really good night out. Girls' nights out evolve over the years.

School discos are replaced by bars and nightclubs, then before long, you start to research quieter restaurants: 'The music's not too loud there so we can have a really good chat.'

We spend so much of our time working and maybe looking after children and generally being too serious about life that we're only too happy to let our hair down and concentrate on the serious business of a fun night out with the girls. Possibly the ultimate getting ready together moment is helping  your best friend on her wedding day. As a bridesmaid, or 'best woman', there is nothing like seeing someone you love transform herself into a stunning, luminous vision on the most

A very merry, dancing, drinking, laughing, quaffing, and unthinking time.

John Dryden

romantic day of her life. Sharing this with her is something you'll never forget. And of course you can sneak in the odd vodka and tonic while you're putting on your clobber. After all, it helps to calm the nerves! Sometimes you're completely out of synch with your friends. They want to go out and party, while you're at home warming babies' bottles. Or else you're both pregnant at the same time and before you know it, the only partying you're doing is booking clowns and making up party bags for kids to take home. If you're lucky you'll both be able to request a pass for an evening – free of children and partners – and enjoy fighting to get a word in edgeways.

'Do you think we'll always do this?' is something many of us have already asked each other. When we're octogenarians, will we still be hanging out together? Will we drink less? Not necessarily! Will we still shake our stuff on the dance floor? Probably not, although Abba's 'Dancing Queen' is always hard to resist. Having a good time with the girls is something you never lose your lust for. How often have you seen a group of grandmothers assembled in a tea room, armed with photos of their grandchildren? Teasing each other, reminiscing and having a ball? Long may the fun continue!

shopping

Retail therapy with female friends

All the money you save by not seeing a shrink can be blown on the things you think you probably don't deserve. Shopping with a friend helps you to process your doubts. You can count on her to say: 'It really suits you! Think of the wear you'll get out of it! It's a long-term investment!' However you deal with

the guilt after the event, at the moment of purchase your friend will be there to egg you on. You begin to believe her when she tells you it's a must-have; a classic. What the hell, it's only money! Perhaps the fun of shopping with a friend allows us to relive those giddy moments years ago when we squeezed into the changing rooms at Top Shop or Miss

A friend is a present you give to yourself.

Robert Louis Stevenson

Selfridge with armfuls of clothes on a Saturday afternoon. Trying on clothes you know you can't afford is pretty pointless when you're on your own, but with a friend, all of a sudden it becomes a worthwhile activity. Later, long after you've put that item out of your mind, your friend might say: 'You know, that sequinned top really did suit you, why don't you go back and get it?' Post-splurge, going through your purchases and debating the best occasion on which each particular item will get its first airing is something best done with friends.

They understand these time-honoured rituals and will always reassure you that you did the right thing. Even if you don't get a chance to shop with your friend any more, you'll still love having the opportunity to talk through an impulse buy with her when you do meet up. And; 'Have you seen those dresses in Jigsaw?' is always a good way of easing yourselves into a full-blown clothes chat. Before you know it, you've made a date to go there together. But it's not just clothes. Browsing in bookshops, going to an antiques market, hankering after kitchens and bathrooms or buying presents for your lover or your children: shopping with a partner in crime can be extremely satisfying. Haggling, finding a bargain and dithering about whether or not you should go back for something can be developed into art forms. The trick is to choose your shopping companions with care.

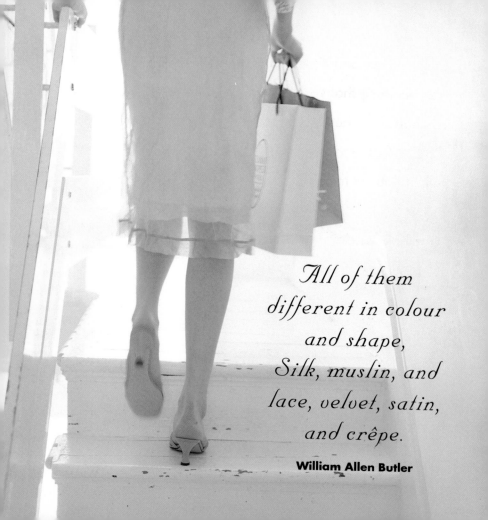

*All of them
different in colour
and shape,
Silk, muslin, and
lace, velvet, satin,
and crêpe.*

William Allen Butler

While one friend might have a talent for assuaging guilt, another could prove to be far too sensible. 'Thank goodness I was there to stop you from shelling out on that stunning dress!' might not always be what you want to hear. When it comes to items such as jewellery, cushions, flowers and all the things you really don't need but admire for their beauty, why not buy them as a gift for your shopping companion? This will give you a guilt free hit. It's always good to have a friend who is an absolute advocate of the power of shopping as a pick-you-up. 'I don't believe in guilt,' she'll say. 'Life's too short!' It's tried and tested: retail therapy soothes the soul and lifts the spirits like nothing else in the world!

life coaching

Friends are the best listeners

There are times when you're really stuck in your life. You might ask your friends for advice. Quite often though, when you start talking things through, all you're actually asking of them is to listen. And as you attempt to tell your story to a good friend, you find yourself learning from it. They help you

to listen to your own voice. How many times have you said to a friend who really understands you, a friend who has a natural gift for listening: 'I feel so much better now that I've talked to you!' Listening to your friends becomes more challenging when you have children. Conversations are constantly interrupted by requests for juice or biscuits.

Mothers learn to develop more advanced listening skills; you need to be able to listen to more than one person at once! Friends are well aware of their role as ongoing listeners – which perhaps explains why they're constantly apologizing for not having been in contact. 'It's been absolutely manic here.' 'Things have been very hectic at work.' 'I can't believe it's nearly June, where does the time go?' Don't feel too guilty. We're all in the same boat. Quite often, when you speak to your friend, you both say: 'I've been thinking about you, I'm just so sorry that I haven't called.' Your friends will always forgive you for having a busy life. Knowing that you're always wishing each other well is brilliant for boosting energy levels when life gets a bit much.

Of all happinesses, the most charming
is that of a firm and gentle friendship.
It sweetens all our cares, dispels our
sorrows, and counsels us in all extremities.

Seneca

And then there are the evenings when you've finally collapsed with a cup of coffee. You're absolutely shattered. The phone rings and for a moment you consider leaving it. But it's the voice of an old friend, and hearing it lifts your spirits. 'I nearly didn't pick up! I'm so glad I did!' And you're off. By the time you put down the phone you feel lighter and younger and so much better! Friends can make wonderful life coaches. What they may lack in objectivity, they make up for in love and concern. And group therapy with friends is to be recommended. By the end of an evening, you've been persuaded to dump the man, leave the job, rent out your flat and buy a round the world ticket, when all you asked, was for some help updating your CV! While you might hesitate when it comes to grasping the nettle, your true friends are the ones who will encourage you to follow your dreams.

I felt it shelter to speak to you.

Emily Dickinson

bliss!

Friends make our lives richer

Without our friends, life would be less interesting, less involving and much less fun. Friends help us to grow. They teach us daring; they infect us with their enthusiasm; thanks to them we are bold. We have the courage to try out new things; to seize the day. They give us the energy we need to experiment, and with their love and support, we have the confidence to develop myriad aspects of our personalities. True friends are willing to embrace change in our lives. The best friends never judge. A flexible friend is a joy to know. She is your steady, faithful companion on your life path. When you meander, go over familiar ground,

Friendship is the inexpressible comfort of feeling safe with a person, having neither to weigh thoughts nor measure words.

George Eliot

or in some cases, start travelling backwards, she understands you, and says, 'Ah, so that's where you are at the moment!' The best friendship is one where each person wants the best for each other. As Aristotle said, true friendship is lasting because it is 'grounded in good'. If you do have this kind of friendship, you know how lucky you are. So while we might often say, 'I don't know what I'd do without her,' can you actually remember the last time you told your friend: 'I don't know what I'd do without you?'

picture credits & acknowledgments

Key: **a**=above, **b**=below, **r**=right, **l**=left, **c**=centre, **ph**= photographer
All photography by **Dan Duchars** taken at Janie Jackson's house in London
(unless stated otherwise)
For specific products contact:
Janie Jackson, Parma Lilac t. 020 8960 9239, f. 020 7912 0993
info@parmalilac.co.uk www.parmalilac.co.uk

3 main ph Ian Wallace **3 inset ph** Debi Treloar; **4 ph** Debi Treloar;
5 ph Catherine Gratwicke/Laura Stoddart's apartment in London; **8 ph** Debi
Treloar; **9 ph** Polly Wreford/Ros Fairman's house in London; **10 ph** Craig
Fordham; **12 ph** Tom Leighton; **14–15 ph** Polly Wreford; **17 ph** James Merrell;
20–21 ph David Brittain; **22 ph** Ian Wallace; **23 ph** Debi Treloar;
26–28 ph Debi Treloar; **32 ph** Polly Wreford/Marie-Hélène de Taillac's pied-à-
terre in Paris; **33 ph** Catherine Gratwicke/Lulu Guinness's home in London;
36 ph Debi Treloar; **37 a ph** Chris Everard; **37 b ph** William Lingwood;
40 l & 40 r ph Polly Wreford; **41–42 ph** Catherine Gratwicke/Lulu Guinness's
home in London; **43 ph** Polly Wreford; **46–47 ph** Caroline Arber;
50–51 ph Sandra Lane; **53 ph** Polly Wreford/travel journal by Darrell Gibbs of
Sukie (www.sukie.co.uk); **54 ph** James Merrell; **57 ph** Debi Treloar;
60–61 ph Polly Wreford/Ros Fairman's house in London

The author would like to thank her friends for contributing to this book.